THE FACTS OF LIFE

Text: René Raff
Illustrations: Georgina Steyn and Ian Anderson
Consultant: Dr Chris Warton

NEW
HOLLAND

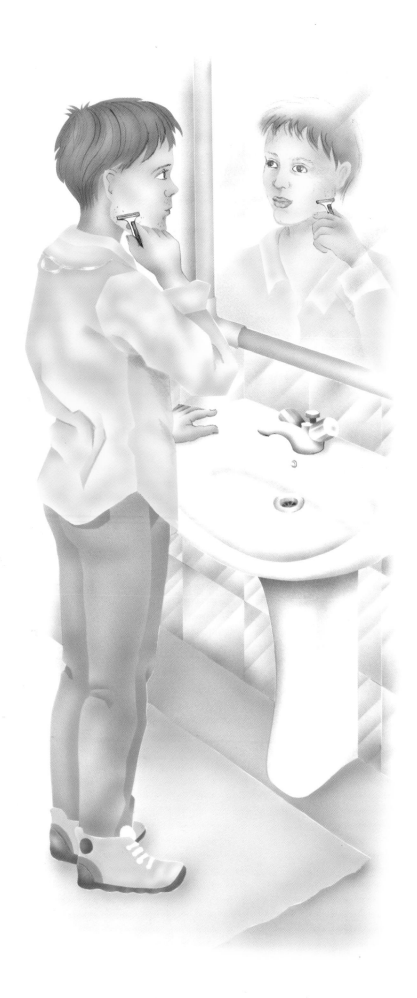

Contents

4. In the beginning

6. Having a baby

8. Welcome to the world

10. Babies

12. Why are we all different?

14. Growing up

16. How our bodies change

18. Girls and puberty

20. Boys and puberty

22. Towards independence

24. In private

26. Finding out about sexuality

28. Contraception

30. Aids and other diseases

32. Index

First published in the UK in 1994 by
New Holland (Publishers) Ltd
London • Cape Town • Sydney • Singapore

Reprinted 1995/1, 1995/2

ISBN 1 85368 356 6

New Holland (Publishers) Ltd
24 Nutford Place, London W1H 6DQ

Editor: Sean Fraser
Designer: Tracey Carstens
Illustrations: Georgina Steyn and Ian Anderson

Typeset by Suzanne Fortescue, Struik DTP
Reproduction by Unifoto (Pty) Ltd
Printed and bound in Singapore by Kyodo Printing Co (Pte) Ltd

Introduction

One of the most fascinating aspects of growing up is learning about the development of the human being, and how our bodies and minds change and grow from the tiniest beginnings into mature and responsible young adults. One of the most exciting times is the teenage years which introduce many important questions, and these answers will help us to understand our developing sexuality, new and undiscovered feelings and the often uncertain move towards independence. The following pages provide an introduction to the facts of life and the many other aspects of growing up. They will help you to understand what happens to you during puberty and provide straightforward and reliable answers to the many questions you may have.

A note to parents

As a parent, you may decide that your own child is not quite ready to appreciate all the issues dealt with in this book. For this reason, you may want to read and discuss each chapter individually with your child, and only present issues once you feel the time is right. Many children are curious about these questions, and in order to encourage a healthy and stable approach to the facts of life, they have a right to an immediate source of information that is both reliable and honest.

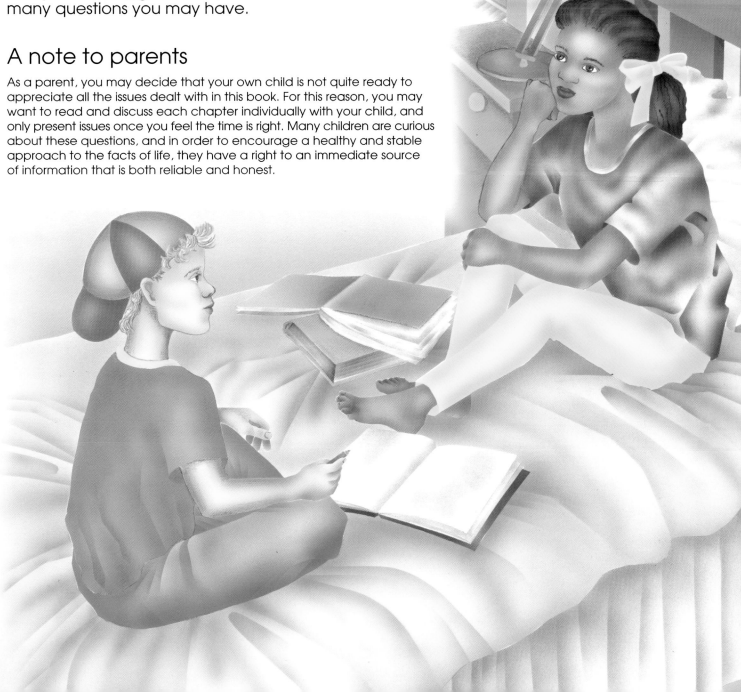

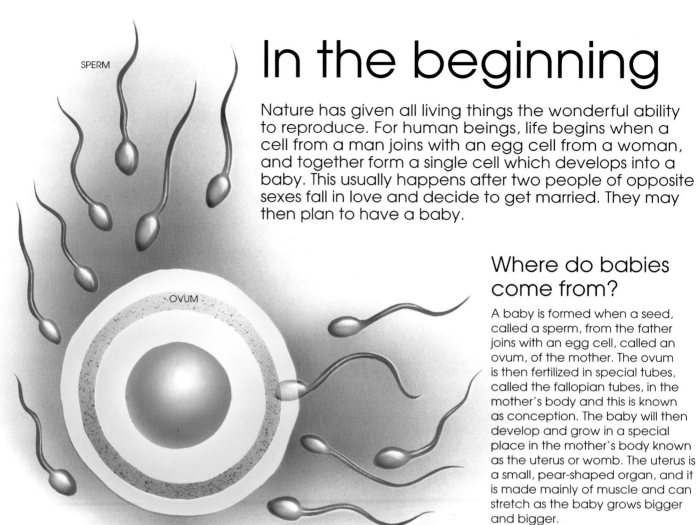

SPERM

OVUM

In the beginning

Nature has given all living things the wonderful ability to reproduce. For human beings, life begins when a cell from a man joins with an egg cell from a woman, and together form a single cell which develops into a baby. This usually happens after two people of opposite sexes fall in love and decide to get married. They may then plan to have a baby.

Where do babies come from?

A baby is formed when a seed, called a sperm, from the father joins with an egg cell, called an ovum, of the mother. The ovum is then fertilized in special tubes, called the fallopian tubes, in the mother's body and this is known as conception. The baby will then develop and grow in a special place in the mother's body known as the uterus or womb. The uterus is a small, pear-shaped organ, and it is made mainly of muscle and can stretch as the baby grows bigger and bigger.

What is an ovum?

An ovum is the female sex cell. It is often called the egg cell and, like a sperm, is so small that it can only be seen through a microscope. When a girl is born, her ovaries (see page 18) already contain hundreds of thousands of ova (the plural of ovum). Once a month from puberty onwards, one of the ovaries will release an ovum. If this ovum is not fertilized by a sperm, it will pass out of the woman's body during menstruation (see page 19).

What is a sperm?

A sperm is the male sex cell which looks a little like a tadpole. It has a head, neck and tail and can swim. Sperm is made and stored in a man's testes (see page 20), and is so tiny that it can only be seen by the human eye if it is placed under a microscope. During sexual intercourse, a man releases a milky-white liquid called semen which contains millions of sperm, but it takes only one sperm to fertilize an ovum.

How does the baby get into the mother's body?

Our parents may express their love for each other in many different ways. One way is through sexual intercourse. Making love, as sexual intercourse is often called, is a private and loving activity during which the father's erect penis (see page 20) is placed inside the mother's vagina (see page 18) and sperm cells are deposited inside her body. These sperm cells swim into the uterus and up into the fallopian tubes where one may meet with the tiny egg from the mother. From this tiny cell, a baby is formed.

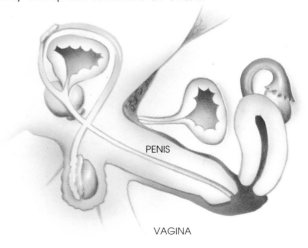

PENIS

VAGINA

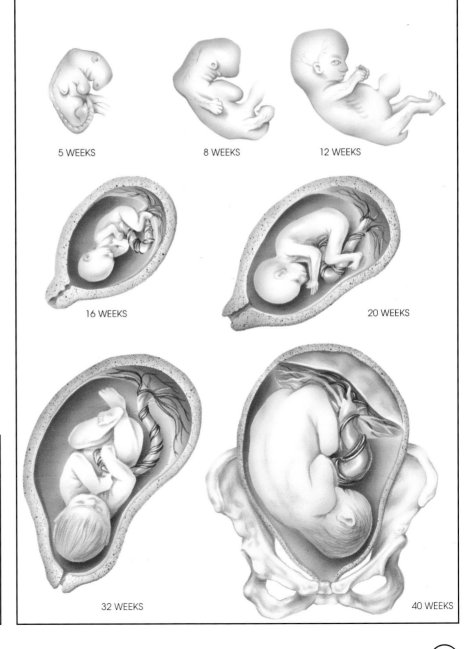

What are the stages of growth?

A human baby takes about 40 weeks from conception to develop into a healthy baby which is ready to enter the world. By the time it is five weeks old, the embryo is still less than one centimetre long, but has a fairly well developed nervous system. At six weeks the head and face can be seen and the fingers, toes, ears and eyes have begun to form. By the end of the eighth week, the embryo is called a fetus and is about three centimetres long By the sixteenth week, the teeth, eyelids and eyelashes have already started to develop and the fetus weighs about 125 grams and is already about 16,5 centimetres long. At this stage, you can tell whether it is a boy or a girl. The heartbeat can be heard after 20 weeks and the mother will be able to feel the thin and wrinkled fetus moving inside her. In about the thirty-second week in the uterus, the fetus starts to get a little fatter and its lungs are almost completely developed. The fetus continues to grow in length and weight until it is about 40 weeks old and usually turns upside down so it is ready to be born.

5 WEEKS   8 WEEKS   12 WEEKS

16 WEEKS   20 WEEKS

32 WEEKS   40 WEEKS

CELL DIVISION

How does a baby start to grow?

The cells in the fertilized ovum divide again and again until a tiny being is formed. This is known as an embryo. At first, it is very small and hardly looks like a human being at all, but the embryo develops quickly and after about six weeks it begins to look like a tiny baby. By the time it is eight weeks old, its body is fully formed and it is known as a fetus.

Did you know?

During her lifetime, a woman's body produces between 300 and 500 egg cells, each of which measures less than one seventh of a millimetre across! And every time a man ejaculates (see page 20 and 21), he releases about 300 million sperm cells, each of which is only about one twentieth of a millimetre long!

Having a baby

Once the mother's ovum has been fertilised by a sperm, a baby starts to develop inside the mother's uterus. We now say that the woman is pregnant.

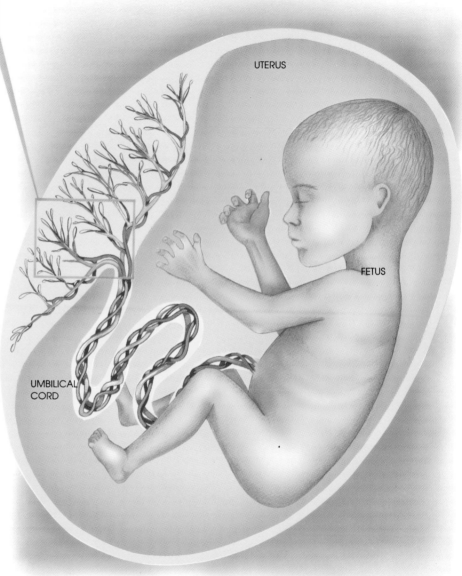

PLACENTA

UTERUS

FETUS

UMBILICAL CORD

Where does the baby get its food while it is growing?

A baby must have food and oxygen, but it cannot eat and breathe by itself. The developing fetus receives food and oxygen from its mother's blood through a tube called the umbilical cord. This cord stretches from the navel of the baby to the placenta. Food and oxygen pass from the mother's blood through the placenta and then down the umbilical cord to the baby. Waste matter from the unborn baby passes back through the cord and placenta into the mother's blood.

What is it like inside the uterus?

After fertilization, a group of spongy blood vessels called the placenta develops inside the uterus. One side of the placenta is attached to the wall of the uterus, while the umbilical cord, which carries food to the fetus, comes out of the other side and is attached to the navel of the fetus. Inside the uterus a thin membrane called an amniotic sac forms a closed bag around the fetus. This is filled with a watery fluid called amniotic fluid. The fetus floats in this fluid which allows it to grow and protects it from any bumps and knocks. The amniotic fluid also helps keep the baby's temperature constant so that the baby does not get too hot or too cold. As the pregnancy progresses, the uterus gets bigger and bigger as the fetus grows.

How long does the baby stay inside its mother's body?

A doctor works out when the baby will be born by calculating the pregnancy from the first day of the mother's last menstrual period. Although it can be shorter or longer, most pregnancies last about 40 weeks, which is equal to about nine months. The development of the fetus may be divided into three stages, called trimesters, and each stage lasts for about three months.

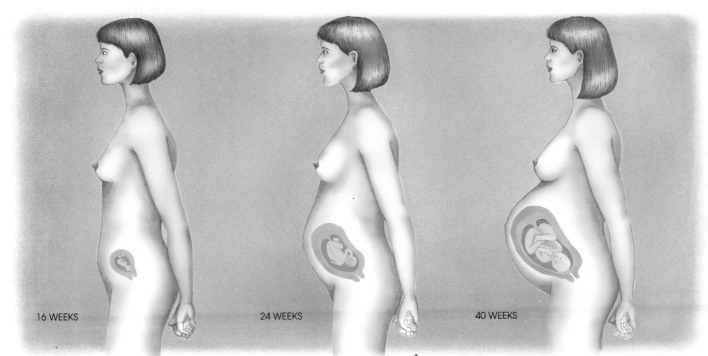

16 WEEKS

24 WEEKS

40 WEEKS

What happens to the mother's body when she is pregnant?

Many changes take place in a woman's body when she is pregnant. Some of these changes are easy to see while others take place inside the mother and affect the functioning of her body. Most of these changes are caused by the hormones, oestrogen and progesterone. Pregnancy does not only affect a woman's reproductive organs. The most obvious change is her big abdomen which expands to accommodate the growing fetus. The hormones cause her breasts to swell and they begin to produce milk. Her ligaments and muscles become softer and more flexible so that the birth process may be easier. The mother may find that the growing baby puts pressure on her bladder and she may have to go to the toilet quite often. Some women may feel clumsy and uncomfortable as their abdomen gets bigger, but despite all these changes in their body, many women feel very well indeed during this exciting time.

What is a miscarriage?

Sometimes something goes wrong with the pregnancy and it ends with the death of the fetus and the loss of the contents of the uterus. This is called a miscarriage. Miscarriages may occur because there is a developmental or genetic problem (see page 13) with the fetus, or the mother's body is unable to keep the pregnancy going due to medical problems. A miscarriage may be the body's way of dealing with defects or serious problems during a pregnancy. Miscarriages are quite common during the first 12 weeks of a baby's development and many women who have had miscarriages, have had very successful pregnancies later on and given birth to healthy babies.

Can anything harm the unborn baby?

Yes. Just as food and oxygen passes from the mother to the baby through the placenta and umbilical cord, harmful drugs and medicines taken by the mother can also affect her baby. These may cause the baby to be born deformed or mentally retarded, so a pregnant woman should not take any medicines which are not prescribed by her doctor. Alcohol and smoking may also harm the developing fetus. The mother's health is very important for the development of the baby. Infections and even a high temperature or fever have been known to affect unborn babies. So a pregnant woman must try to eat the right food and rest as much as she can. She also needs to take special tablets which contain iron, vitamins and minerals to help her and her baby to stay healthy.

ALCOHOL

DRUGS

Welcome to the world

After carrying the growing baby inside her for nine months, the mother is ready to give birth. Having a baby can be a very exciting experience for the mother and the father. Medical science has developed ways of helping to make the birth of a baby easier and safer.

What happens when the baby is ready to be born?

The strong muscles of the mother's uterus start to contract and she may have cramps. This is called labour and the contractions become stronger and more regular as the labour progresses. The opening of the uterus, which is also called the cervix, has to stretch to about ten centimetres to allow the baby to pass from the uterus into the vagina and this may take between two and twelve hours. There is pressure on the amniotic sac (see page 6), and it breaks and the fluid runs out of the mother's body.

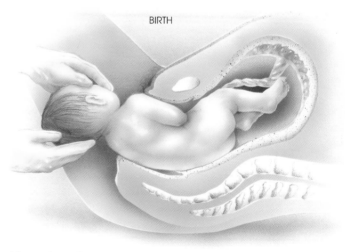

BIRTH

FETUS AT
40 WEEKS

How does the baby get out of the mother's body?

The vagina, which leads from the outside of the mother's body to her uterus, is quite a narrow passage but as the baby passes down it, it stretches to let the baby pass through. Each time the muscles in her uterus contract, the mother has to push until the baby's head emerges from the vaginal opening. The baby is still attached to the placenta inside the mother's body by the umbilical cord and once the baby has been born the cord is cut and then clamped. The placenta detaches itself from the uterus and passes out of the mother's body. This is sometimes called the 'afterbirth'. After the birth the passage shrinks to its original size.

Did you know?

Boys are usually bigger than girls – even at birth! Full term baby boys weigh about 3,6 kilograms when they are born and baby girls weigh about 3,2 kilograms. Most newborn babies are about 50 centimetres long.

Is there any pain during labour?

Yes, there can be, but there are ways of making labour less painful and more comfortable for the mother. Sometimes the mother is given an injection in her lower back so that the lower half of her body becomes numb and she feels no pain. This is called an epidural and may be used for caesarian sections. The mother is then able to stay awake and participate in the birth of her baby. Sometimes the mother is given a mixture of oxygen and nitrous oxide (laughing gas) to breathe while she has her contractions. Many pregnant women go to special classes where they are taught breathing exercises so their labour is not as painful.

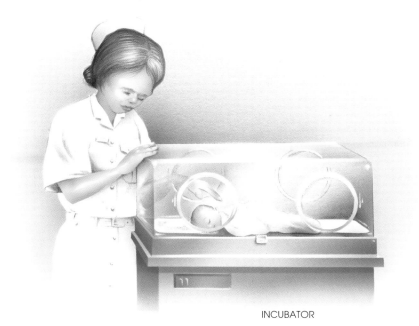

INCUBATOR

Are all babies born the same way?

No, most babies are born head first but sometimes the buttocks come out first and this is then called a breech delivery. If necessary, metal 'spoons' called forceps may be placed around the baby's head to help pull it out more quickly, or a suction device may be attached to the top of the baby's head for the same reason. A cut, called an episiotomy, may be made at the opening of the vagina to prevent the mother's skin from tearing or a delay in the birth which could harm the baby.

What is a caesarian section?

Sometimes it is necessary to deliver the baby by means of an operation. A small cut is made through the mother's abdomen and into her uterus. This is usually done if the baby needs to be delivered quickly or if the mother's pelvic area, or hips, are too small for the baby to pass through. The Roman emperor Julius Caesar was said to have been born this way and so the operation is now called a caesarian section.

Why are some babies put into an incubator?

Sometimes babies are born too early and cannot survive without the help of machines and medicines. These babies are called premature babies and they are usually born between the 28th and 37th week of the pregnancy. They are often very small and weak, and their lungs may not yet work properly. Premature babies and those born by caesarian section may be placed in a closed, transparent crib called an incubator. Here they are kept warm and are given extra oxygen to help them breathe. They may also be fed through special tubes to help them grow.

Why do babies cry when they are born?

While in the uterus the fetus gets the oxygen it needs from its mother, and its airways are filled with amniotic fluid. This fluid is usually squeezed out of the baby's lungs during labour. When the baby is born it takes its first breath of air, usually by crying, and its lungs then expand so that the baby can breathe on its own.

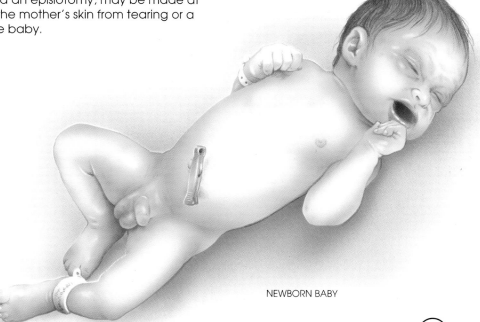

NEWBORN BABY

Babies

The miracle of birth is one of life's great wonders and may bring great joy to a family. Although most newborn babies may look alike, they are all very different and every baby grows in its own special way to become an independent human being.

BREASTFEEDING

Can new babies see?

Newborn babies can only see objects which are very close to them and no further than about 20 centimetres away. As they grow and develop, their sight improves so they can focus on objects all around them. Most babies start recognising their parents' faces when they are between six and eight weeks old.

When can babies start eating solid food?

Some babies only start eating solid food when they are about six months old, while others start eating at three months and some even before that. The first solid food a baby eats is usually one or two teaspoonfuls of baby cereal and this amount is slowly increased over time. Gradually, other foods which have been well mashed are given to the growing baby. When the baby is seven or eight months old, it can start to chew coarser foods. It is very important that the baby eats simple and nourishing foods to help it grow.

What do new babies eat?

For the first few months of their lives, milk is all the food babies will need. From just before the baby is born, a clear substance called colostrum is produced from the mother's breasts. The colostrum is high in protein and has important antibodies to help babies fight off infection. Two or three days after her baby has been born, the mother's breasts start to produce milk. A mother's breast milk is easily digested and is regarded by many people as the best for babies. Some mothers choose not to breast feed and prefer to give their babies special milk formulas. Most new babies need to be fed every three to four hours.

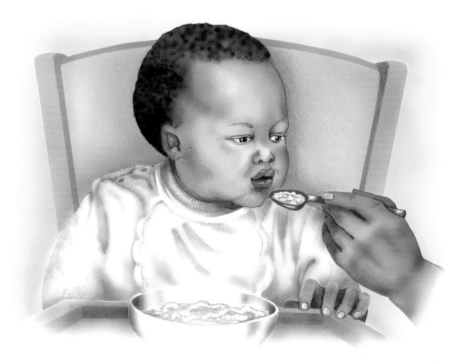

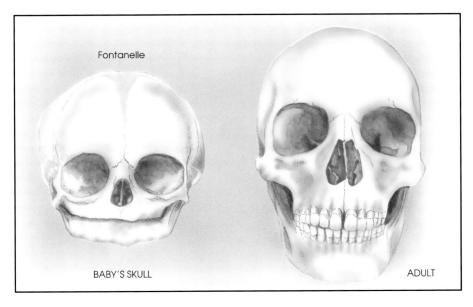

Fontanelle

BABY'S SKULL   ADULT

Do babies really have soft skulls?

No, but there are several soft areas on top of the baby's head called fontanelles. These occur where the skull bones have not yet grown or fused together. Some of these areas may grow closed within about three weeks, but the largest fontanelle on the top of the skull takes about a year to close properly. Until this happens this area on the baby's head will feel soft.

What are birth marks?

A birth mark is often little more than a discoloration of the skin and is usually quite harmless. Although some disappear on their own, others are permanent. Most birth marks are caused by widened blood vessels under the surface of the skin and are therefore red or blue. Other spots may be caused by a collection of pigment and these are usually brown and may be permanent.

What happens during the baby's first year?

A human baby is quite helpless when it is born. When the baby is about five weeks old it begins to show some interest in its surroundings. In the first year the baby will learn to roll over, sit, grasp, crawl, stand and finally walk alone. At about nine months, a baby may begin to communicate, and starts babbling simple words such as Mama or Dada. By the time it is about one year old it may understand simple questions and commands. Physically, the baby will have its permanent eye colour, about 12 teeth and most of its hair. A healthy full term baby should be three times its birth weight and about 75 centimetres tall by the end of the first year, and the little person begins to develop an individual personality.

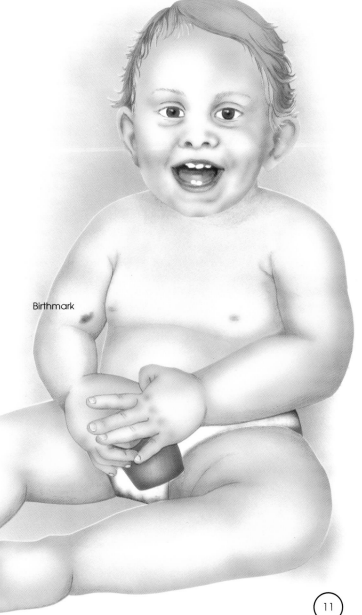

Birthmark

Why are we all different?

As children grow up, they all go through similar stages of physical and mental development, but no two human beings are ever the same. Every person is unique and has an individual personality and features. These are formed by the genes received from their parents.

What are chromosomes?

These are strands of chemicals folded up in the centre of each of the body's cells. There are 46 chromosomes in each cell and each chromosome contains thousands of genes. Chromosomes carry all the information needed to make more cells and all the important substances such as proteins and hormones which are needed to keep the human body healthy and working properly.

CHROMOSOMES ARE LIKE LONG, TWISTED LADDERS

What are genes?

A gene is the microscopic part of a chromosome responsible for giving us our individual characteristics. We inherit genes from our parents and they determine aspects such as our blood type, height, and the colour of our hair and eyes. They may also affect our individual personality and even our intelligence.

Why do we look like our parents?

Half of the genes we have come from our mother and the other half from our father, so features such as the colour of our eyes, for example, are passed on from our parents. These features may change slightly because they mix with the genes of each of our parents. Sometimes a feature not seen in either a mother or a father, but which is very obvious in a grandparent, may be found in a child. This shows us that that genes are in fact passed down from one generation to the next.

CHROMOSOMES IN THE CELL NUCLEUS CONTAIN GENES

What is a hereditary disease?

A disease which is inherited from our parents. Genes are passed on from generation to generation. In this way, a group of genes causing the illness is able to stay within the family line. Some of these diseases may only be found in boys, while some may only affect every second or third generation. But not every child from a family with a history of such a disease will be affected. Tests can be done on an unborn baby to check whether it has inherited any of these diseases from its parents.

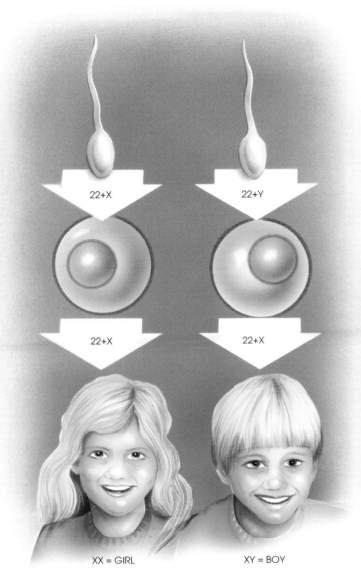

XX = GIRL   XY = BOY

How do you get twins?

When a mother produces two separate ova at the same time and both are fertilized by the father's sperm, she will give birth to non-identical twins. Each baby will have developed in its own amniotic sac (see page 6) and may not even look like the other. Non-identical twins may be either boys or girls, or even one of each. Identical twins are not as common and develop from the same fertilized egg which splits in half. Identical twins will always be the same sex.

What if something goes wrong?

Ova and sperm have only 23 chromosomes each. Sometimes something goes wrong when a fertilized cell starts to divide (see page 5) and the baby might receive more or less than the 23 chromosomes from one parent. This extra or missing chromosome will affect the development of the embryo and the baby will be born with an abnormality. An example of this is Down's Syndrome, sometimes called mongolism.

What makes the baby a boy or a girl?

The baby's sex is determined the moment the father's sperm fertilizes the mother's ovum. The sex genes are carried on chromosomes called X and Y. It is the father who determines the sex of the baby because sperm cells have either an X or a Y chromosome, while an egg cell has only an X chromosome. A baby with two Xs will be a girl, while one with an X and a Y will be a boy.

IDENTICAL TWINS

NON-IDENTICAL TWINS

Did you know?

Siamese twins occur when a fertilized ovum splits to form identical twins, but the cell does not separate properly. Siamese twins are joined together and share some part of their bodies, but some may be separated in an operation. We call these babies 'Siamese twins' after the twin boys, Chang and Eng, who were born in Siam in 1811 and who were joined together at the chest.

Growing up

As the baby develops into a child and then into an adult, physical changes begin to take place. The shape of the body changes, and both weight and height increase. But there are also very important changes which are less obvious. The young person begins to mature and learns to be responsible and independent. This is all part of the process of growing up.

What are the stages of growing up?

A child develops very quickly in the first two years of life. Many new skills are learnt and the toddler begins to develop an individual personality. Between the ages of three and five, the young person begins to interact with other children, and learns to play and share. The preschooler is constantly learning about people, and it is usually at this stage that the child realizes that boys and girls are different from each other. School will then introduce the child to many new experiences. Although the child's body does not change very much between the ages of six and 12 years, it continues to grow steadily and prepares for the changes that will happen during the teenage years.

Do I change as I grow up?

Yes, you do. Not only are you capable of many new physical skills, but as you grow up you are more able to make your own mature decisions. You will find that you can communicate and express yourself more clearly. Becoming more independent (see page 22) is one of the most exciting changes during these years and it is often a challenge to be able to do and learn new things. But sometimes this new independence may cause a few problems in the home, so it is important to remember that even though you are growing up and changing, you still need adult guidance and need to obey the rules laid down by your parents.

How much sleep do we need?

The amount of sleep people need varies, and as you grow older you will need considerably less sleep. Young children and even teenagers usually need between 10 and 12 hours sleep a night, but older people may only need about eight hours sleep. Sleep is very important for good health and helps keep us both alert and active, so we should always make sure that we get a good night's rest – especially if we are studying for a test or exam, or preparing for sport events.

Why is personal hygiene so important?

During the teenage years, your skin and sweat glands produce substances which may cause unpleasant body odours, so it is very important to bath or shower regularly. It will also be especially necessary to wash thoroughly around the genitals and under your arms – areas where you tend to sweat more during puberty. It may also be necessary for both boys and girls to start using a deodorant. Your hair may become more greasy and may need to be washed more often than before. It is good to take pride in your body and keep yourself clean and healthy.

Is food and exercise really important?

It is always important to have a balanced diet. This is especially true when growing up and during puberty, when your body needs fuel and energy to accommodate all the changes it is going through. Fresh fruit and vegetables, dairy products, meat, fish and eggs provide us with all the essential nutrients important for healthy development. Exercise strengthens our bones and muscles, and helps with co-ordination and muscle development. Regular exercise is not only fun and important, but also helps us to relax.

What is an eating disorder?

Some people eat too much and become too fat, while others may eat too little and become too thin. This obsessive behaviour is known as an eating disorder, and often affects young people who may have some difficulty dealing with social or emotional problems. Young girls may suffer from serious eating disorders such as anorexia or bulimia, and this is quite common during the teenage years. Being sensible about eating the right food and being comfortable with yourself and your body image is a way of avoiding these serious illnesses.

When do I stop growing?

Most people are fully grown by the time they are 18 years old, but the rate of growth varies considerably from person to person and even between the sexes. Some people only start growing in their late teens, while others may be fully grown by the time they are 15 years old. 'Early' or 'late' starters may at first feel out of place among their peers, but although this is sometimes difficult to accept, all these variations are really quite normal.

How our bodies change

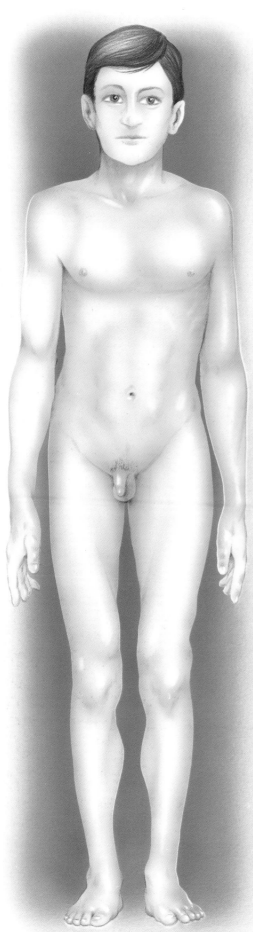

Puberty is an exciting, but sometimes uncertain time. This is the stage when a boy begins to change into a man and a girl into a woman. Puberty can occur at any time between the ages of 10 and 17 years and involves both physical and emotional change.

Why is puberty so important to our development?

Puberty is caused by the sex hormones and is the beginning of the teenage years and adolescence. Once puberty begins we start to become adults – not only in our bodily functions and appearance, but also in our feelings and ideas. Our bodies begin to change internally and externally and we become capable of reproduction. During puberty, most young people start thinking more about the opposite sex and would like to appear attractive to them. After puberty a person is physically and sexually mature.

What are hormones?

Hormones are chemicals in the body which are produced by a group of glands known as the endocrine glands. The many different types of hormones affect different parts of our bodies and control factors such as growth, sexual development, digestion, and many other important bodily functions. The sex hormones control sexual growth and development during puberty and they are also responsible for the sexual functions of both men and women long after puberty has ended. The main female sex hormones are oestrogen and progesterone, while the main male sex hormone is testosterone.

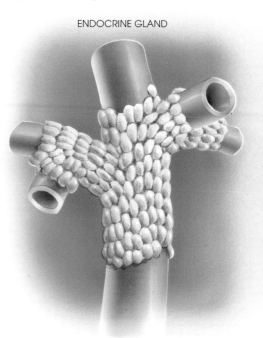

ENDOCRINE GLAND

What are the changes boys experience?

During puberty a boy's shoulders and chest become broader and he usually becomes heavier and more muscular than girls. Pubic hair begins to develop, and hair also grows under the arms, on the chest and limbs, and even on the face. Not only will most boys have to start shaving at this point, but their faces will also begin to change shape, and they too will begin to look more adult. The larynx, or voice box, grows and the voice becomes deeper. The male genitals grow bigger and start to produce sperm. A boy is then able to ejaculate and may also experience nocturnal emissions, or wet dreams (see page 21).

How do girls change during puberty?

Puberty, in both girls and boys, usually starts with a sudden growth spurt in which our arms and legs grow and our hands and feet get bigger. Hair also begins to grow under the arms and in the genital area. Hair in the genital area is called pubic hair. A girl's face changes so that she looks more grown up, and oestrogen makes the skin on her face softer. Breast development begins and her genitals get bigger. The shape of the girl's body also changes and her hips become wider to make room for a growing baby during pregnancy. The hormones trigger the production of ova and the girl experiences her first menstrual period (see page 19).

Do boys and girls reach puberty at the same time?

No, they do not. Girls usually reach puberty one to two years earlier than most boys. The average age is usually between 11 and 12 years for girls, while most boys reach puberty between 13 and 14 years.

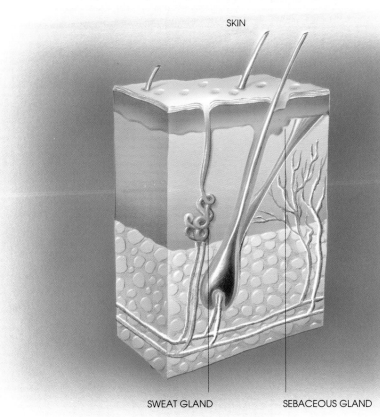

SKIN

SWEAT GLAND   SEBACEOUS GLAND

Can we expect any other changes?

Yes. Your body sweats much more during puberty – even if you have not exerted yourself. Anxiety, excitement and nervousness will may also cause you to sweat unexpectedly. Because sebaceous glands in the skin produce more sebum, an oily substance which can block the pores, some people develop pimples during puberty. Do not pick at these pimples but rather keep the skin clean and visit a doctor if you are worried. Sometimes all these changes happen quite fast, and you may begin to feel self-conscious and uncomfortable – particularly in the company of people of the opposite sex. It may take a while to get used to your new body, but it is important that you try to feel good about yourself.

Girls and puberty

During puberty a girl's body begins to look and even feel different. Sometimes a girl may not even be aware of the changes in her body, but at other times these changes may be quite obvious. To help her feel confident and happy about these changes, a girl needs to understand the female reproductive system and how it works.

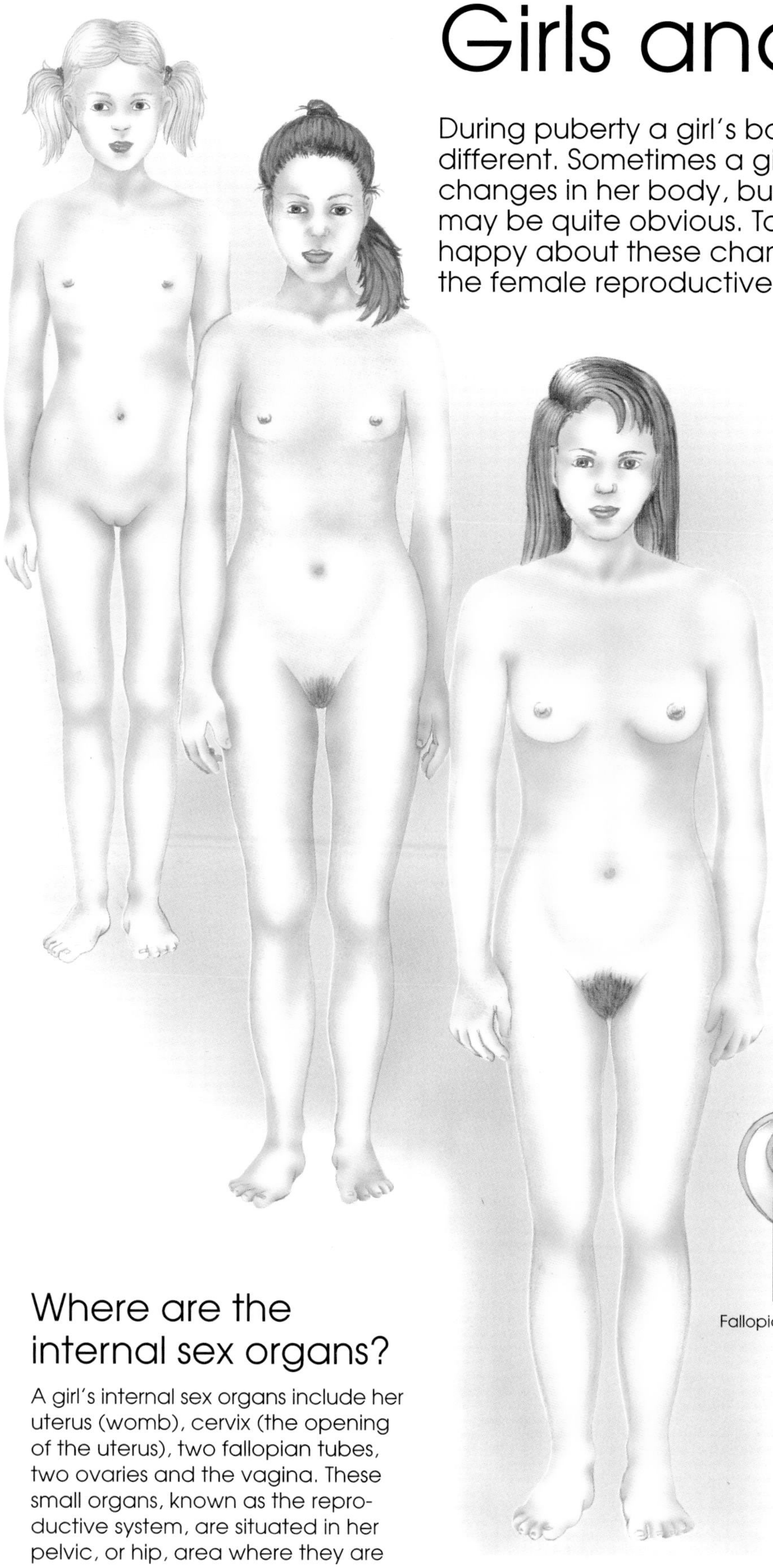

Where are a girl's external sex organs?

A girl's external sex organs, or genitals, are sometimes called the vulva. They are tucked away between her legs and are not easily seen. They consist of a highly sensitive organ called the clitoris, and two pairs of skin folds called the outer labia and the inner labia. This is the area where pubic hair (see page 17) starts to grow during puberty. There are also two small, but separate openings, and each has its own function. Urine passes out of the smaller opening, called the urethra, which leads from the urinary system. The opening leading to the internal sex organs is the vaginal opening. At the vaginal opening there is a ring of tissue called the hymen (see page 27).

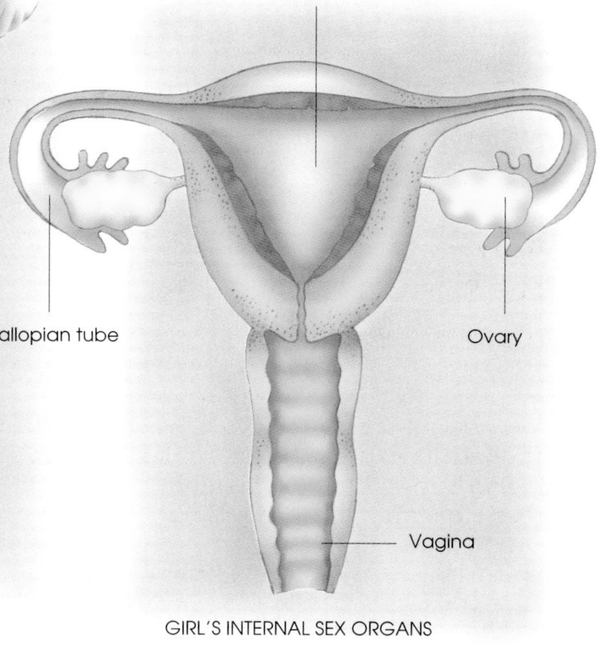

Uterus

Fallopian tube

Ovary

Vagina

GIRL'S INTERNAL SEX ORGANS

Where are the internal sex organs?

A girl's internal sex organs include her uterus (womb), cervix (the opening of the uterus), two fallopian tubes, two ovaries and the vagina. These small organs, known as the reproductive system, are situated in her pelvic, or hip, area where they are protected by the bones of the pelvis.

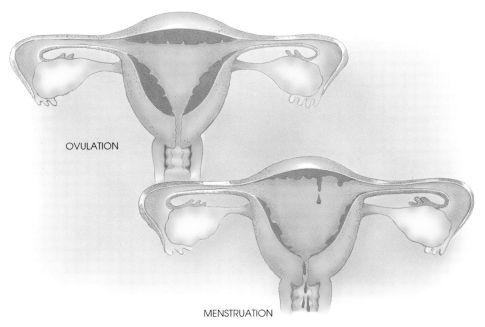

OVULATION

MENSTRUATION

Am I ready to have a baby now?

No, you are not. Although the onset of menstruation means that a girl's body is able to reproduce, having a baby is an enormous responsibility and involves much more than just physical maturity. There are many other important issues which need to be considered. Emotional stability, a stable relationship, such as marriage, and financial security are just some of the factors which will help you become a happy and confident parent. A teenage pregnancy may also carry risks to the health of both the young mother and the baby.

How does menstruation affect my body?

Menstruation is a completely normal and healthy part of every woman's life. Although the average menstrual cycle is about 28 days, it can be anything from 25 to 35 days. Some women have regular cycles and know exactly when to expect their next period, while others have irregular cycles. Most young girls have irregular cycles in the beginning as their bodies get used to the hormones they are producing, and it can take about a year for the cycle to become regular. During menstruation, some girls may experience cramps in the lower back and pelvic area. These occur because the muscles of the uterus contract to expel the lining. In most cases these cramps are not too severe, but some women have very painful and heavy periods, and may even need to visit a doctor. Sanitary towels or tampons which are used to absorb the menstrual blood must be changed regularly. Menstruation should in no way change your lifestyle, and you can continue to do everything you normally do.

What is menstruation?

Menstruation, which you may call your 'periods', is the monthly shedding of blood from the uterus. It is part of a process known as the menstrual cycle which is controlled by the sex hormones and begins at puberty. During the cycle, the lining of the uterus, called the endometrium, becomes thicker and an egg, or ovum, is produced. If the egg is not fertilized by sperm, the lining of the uterus is not needed and it breaks down and passes out of the girl's body with the menstrual blood. The menstrual cycle usually occurs about every 28 days and lasts for about three to seven days. Anxiety, stress, loss of weight and a change in routine can affect the cycle and cause a period to come earlier, later or be missed altogether. A missed period may also be a sign of pregnancy.

Why are girls concerned about the size of their breasts?

Because breasts are a particular female characteristic, many girls relate the size of their breasts to their attractiveness as a woman. During puberty the development of a girl's breasts is the most obvious change. The most important function of the breasts is to provide milk for feeding babies. There are so many shapes and sizes of breasts, but this has nothing to do with either the ability of one day feeding your own baby or your attractiveness to men. The size of your breasts is part of who you are and makes you unique. Rather than worry about them accept your breasts as part of your own special attraction.

CROSS-SECTION THROUGH THE BREAST

Boys and puberty

Puberty and the process of becoming a man may take time and bring with it some uncertainty and anxiety. Understanding all the changes his body is going through may help a boy make the sometimes difficult transition from childhood to manhood.

Where are a man's sex organs?

Although a woman's most important sex organs are found internally, a man's genitals are situated outside his body. The penis consists of a long shaft and sensitive tip called the glans, which is covered by a fold of skin called the foreskin. At the base of the penis is a loose pouch of skin called the scrotum which contains the testes. The testes are two small, spherical organs which produce sperm (see page 4). Two sperm ducts run from the testes into the urethra which is a long tube running down the shaft of the penis to its tip. The urethra carries urine from the bladder to the outside of the body and, during sexual excitement, sperm also leaves the man's body through this tube. A man also has two small organs, called the prostate gland and the seminal vesicles, which produce seminal fluid.

How does an erection occur?

Erections occur as a result of increased blood flow to the tissues of the penis. This causes the shaft of the penis to become stiff and erect and usually happens during some sort of sexual stimulation. Boys are able to have erections from birth, but they become more frequent from puberty onwards. Erections can be triggered either by a sexy thought or looking at a sexy picture. Some men may wake up with an erection in the morning, but this is usually caused by the pressure of a full bladder and is quite normal.

Did you know?

The testes can only produce sperm at 35° Celsius which is 2 degrees cooler than normal body temperature. Because the temperature outside is cooler, the testes hang in the scrotum outside the body.

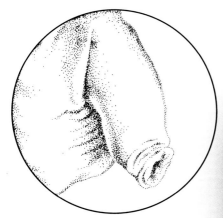

UNCIRCUMCISED PENIS

Why are some boys circumcised?

There may be many different reasons for circumcision, which is the surgical removal of the foreskin from the penis. Some religions, such as the Muslim and Jewish faiths, for example, require infant boys to be circumcised. Circumcision makes no difference to the male sexual act, but is considered by many to be more hygienic.

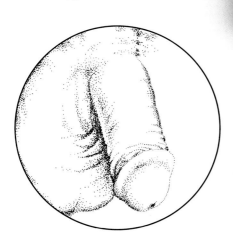

CIRCUMCISED PENIS

Testis

Penis

Urethra

BOY'S SEX ORGANS

How does sperm leave the man's body?

From puberty onwards boys are not only able to have erections, but they also become capable of ejaculation. Ejaculation is the squirting out of sperm from the penis and is a sign that the man is able to reproduce. This happens at the peak of sexual excitement and is sometimes called orgasm. At the point of ejaculation, sperm moves from the testes upwards, picking up seminal fluid from the seminal vesicle and prostate gland. Seminal fluid helps the sperm flow easier and supplies it with nutrients. The sperm mixed with seminal fluid is now called semen and moves through the urethra and is ejaculated from the man's body. The process takes a few seconds to occur.

What is a wet dream?

Sometimes a boy may ejaculate while he is sleeping. This is called a nocturnal emission, but is also known as a wet dream. Some boys actually wake up when they have wet dreams, while others find their sheets damp in the morning. Wet dreams may be caused by sexy dreams, but a boy may not even remember dreaming at all. Wet dreams are a normal part of growing up. They are the body's way of dealing with its new function of producing sperm. Some teenage boys report having regular wet dreams, while others may never experience them. This variation is completely normal.

Is the size of the penis important?

Just as other body parts vary in size from person to person, so does the size of the penis. While in the limp or flaccid state, sizes seem to vary, but when erect, most penises are about the same size. It is not true that a man with a bigger penis is more masculine or manly than one with a smaller penis. The size of a penis does not affect the amount of sexual pleasure or sexual ability of either the man or the woman.

Towards independence

Becoming a teenager means being more independent, choosing your own friends and even making your own decisions. Independence seems so adult and exciting, but it also means that we should behave sensibly and responsible, and not allow ourselves to be pressured into doing something we may later regret.

Why do I sometimes feel happy and other times so miserable?

This is very much a part of adolescence and is caused by both mental and physical changes. Many young people are anxious about growing up, about being 'normal' and being accepted and liked by parents, peers, teachers and others. Although this is completely normal, it can cause a great deal of insecurity and unhappiness which may lead to moodiness and temper outbursts. As we grow older we learn to deal with these feelings and express ourselves in a more rational way. Luckily, this confusing time passes and is replaced by happy, active times. You will learn to accept yourself, and make new and mature plans for the future.

What is peer pressure?

Peers are people at a similar age and stage as you are. The peer group becomes very important during the adolescent years as it provides a feeling of security and belonging. Being with peers also gives a teenager the chance to learn to communicate and interact with equals. Most teenagers do not want to be different from others in their group and so they may do things they would not normally do. The influence peers have over each other is known as 'peer pressure' and can become quite negative, especially for a young person who is not yet mature enough to be able to say 'no'.

How do I say no?

It is not always easy for a teenager to say no. This is because there is always the fear of losing friends. Part of the process of growing up is developing your own point of view and learning to make decisions about matters which affect you. A real friend will respect your decisions and the whole group will admire you for sticking to what you believe is right. Saying 'no' may become easier if you try to avoid situations in which you feel uncomfortable and under pressure.

Is smoking and drinking alcohol dangerous?

Yes. Both alcohol and cigarettes contain dangerous and even addictive substances which do a great deal of damage to the body, particularly to the body of a growing teenager. Many young people associate smoking and drinking with being adult and sophisticated, and a way to impress our friends or feel part of a group. Some shy teenagers find that alcohol relaxes them and allows them to cope with insecurity, but alcohol is in fact a chemical substance which slows down responses and affects judgement and co-ordination. The effects of alcohol abuse on our health soon become very clear, and although the effects of smoking are more long-term, cigarettes are no less dangerous. There is a definite link between smoking and major health problems such as cancer and heart attacks.

HEALTHY LUNG CELLS

DAMAGED LUNG CELLS

Does my appearance matter?

Most teenagers are very concerned about their physical appearance. They may see what they wear as a way of either declaring their independence, or of fitting into their peer group. They may do this by wearing either fashionable or even unconventional clothes. Either way, many young people (and some older people too) choose clothes which make a statement about themselves or the way they feel. Being untidy may cause some conflict at home, but looking presentable will give you confidence in both adult and peer group company.

How will my attitude change?

As you grow older you will begin to form your own ideas and values. By discussing things with your parents and other adults, you will come to your own conclusions. Sometimes you will agree but at other times you may disagree. A sign of maturity is being able to deal with differences in a constructive way, rather than shouting, screaming and slamming the door. Remember, you are on your way to adulthood. Think about issues that are important to you. This will allow you to to be more comfortable with yourself and your feelings.

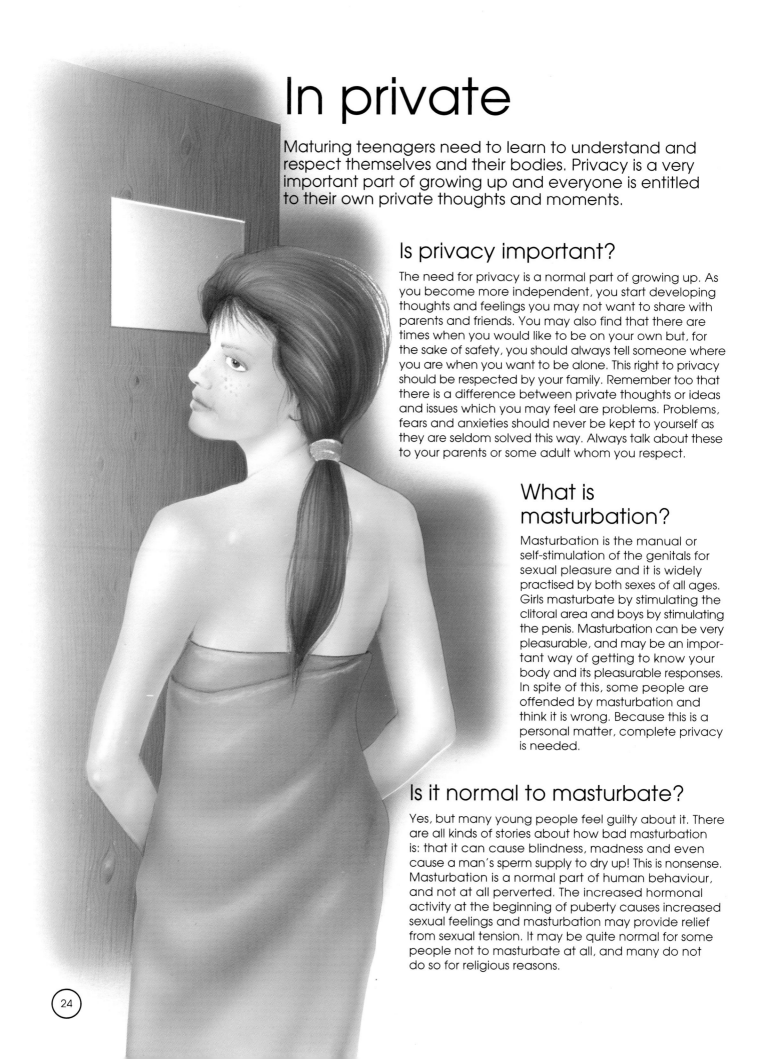

In private

Maturing teenagers need to learn to understand and respect themselves and their bodies. Privacy is a very important part of growing up and everyone is entitled to their own private thoughts and moments.

Is privacy important?

The need for privacy is a normal part of growing up. As you become more independent, you start developing thoughts and feelings you may not want to share with parents and friends. You may also find that there are times when you would like to be on your own but, for the sake of safety, you should always tell someone where you are when you want to be alone. This right to privacy should be respected by your family. Remember too that there is a difference between private thoughts or ideas and issues which you may feel are problems. Problems, fears and anxieties should never be kept to yourself as they are seldom solved this way. Always talk about these to your parents or some adult whom you respect.

What is masturbation?

Masturbation is the manual or self-stimulation of the genitals for sexual pleasure and it is widely practised by both sexes of all ages. Girls masturbate by stimulating the clitoral area and boys by stimulating the penis. Masturbation can be very pleasurable, and may be an important way of getting to know your body and its pleasurable responses. In spite of this, some people are offended by masturbation and think it is wrong. Because this is a personal matter, complete privacy is needed.

Is it normal to masturbate?

Yes, but many young people feel guilty about it. There are all kinds of stories about how bad masturbation is: that it can cause blindness, madness and even cause a man's sperm supply to dry up! This is nonsense. Masturbation is a normal part of human behaviour, and not at all perverted. The increased hormonal activity at the beginning of puberty causes increased sexual feelings and masturbation may provide relief from sexual tension. It may be quite normal for some people not to masturbate at all, and many do not do so for religious reasons.

Is it wrong to want to bath alone?

No, not at all. As a child you may often have bathed with a brother or sister, or even your mother or father, but as you grow older you may see bath time as a time to be on your own. The changes your body goes through during puberty may make you shy and no-one should make you feel at all uncomfortable about your naked body. Bath time is also a quiet opportunity to think about the day's activities and to gather your thoughts together while on your own – without being disturbed by the rest of your family. Although privacy may mean relaxing in hot bath, remember that other members of the family may also want to use the bathroom!

What is sexual abuse?

When someone touches your body and genitals when you don't want them to, or forces you to have sexual intercourse, this is called sexual abuse. Unfortunately, some adults are confused about their sexuality and have serious sexual problems which may affect other people. A paedophile, for example, is an adult who is sexually attracted to children. It is a very serious crime for any adult to take sexual advantage of a child or teenager and it is important to tell someone you trust immediately. Never keep this kind of abuse a secret – no matter who the person is or how much you are being threatened to keep silent. Remember, it is never your fault so you should never feel guilty about it.

What is pornography?

Pornography is the explicit portrayal of human sex in a way that is meant to be stimulating. It is something which offends many people as it allows a private act between two people to be distributed in the form of magazines, photographs, movies and videos. While many young people (and even some older people too) may be curious about pornography, it is important to remember that it serves no purpose at all other than to present sexuality in an unacceptable and vulgar way.

Is rape a crime?

Yes, it is a very serious and violent crime! Rape is the most extreme invasion of privacy a person can experience and a rapist can face a long prison sentence. Men who rape have no respect for their victims and prey on innocent people, and sometimes even on children. Everyone has the right to say 'no' to sexual intercourse, and anyone who ignores that right and forces someone to have sex is a criminal who deserves to be punished. If you think you need to talk to a rape counsellor turn to page 31 for more information.

Finding out about sexuality

Our sexuality, and how we feel about being male or female, is a very important part of who we are. These feelings should be good because when we feel positive about ourselves, our relationships with other people are much more rewarding.

Is it normal to think about the opposite sex so often?

Yes, most teenagers spend a lot of time thinking about the opposite sex. Daydreams and fantasies are perfectly normal and are a result of increased sex hormone levels produced by the hypothalamus and pituitary gland in the brain. The desire for physical contact with the opposite sex may be very strong as sexual feelings develop.

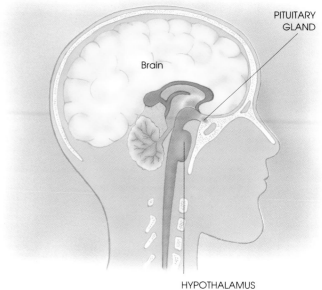

PITUITARY GLAND

Brain

HYPOTHALAMUS

Do my parents understand the changes I am going through?

Although it is difficult for some parents to accept that their children are developing into individuals with their own ideas and feelings, most parents do understand – even though they seem reluctant to talk about sexual matters. All parents went through exactly the same changes which you are undergoing, so whenever you have a question or a problem to discuss, always go to them first. Your parents will give you mature advice even if you do not always agree with them! Remember, too, that many of the stories you hear from your friends, especially about sex, may be completely untrue, so if you are still unsure about certain facts, then maybe a teacher or adult who you respect will be able to help you.

When will I be ready to have sex?

Most young people are curious about sex. Sex is often the subject of jokes and is shown in a rather easygoing way in movies and on television. This sort of casual sex creates the wrong impression. We should always think of sex as being part of a loving, mature and committed relationship. While there are strong sexual feelings during the teenage years, sexual intercourse during these years of development involves many emotional and physical risks.

What is a virgin?

A virgin is a person who has never had sexual intercourse. There is no way of telling whether a man has had intercourse or not. But women have a ring of tissue, called a hymen (see page 18), at the opening of the vagina and when the hymen is torn or stretched, this may mean that she is sexually active. Remember too, however, that this may not always be the case as the hymen may have been stretched or torn in other ways, such as during physical exercise.

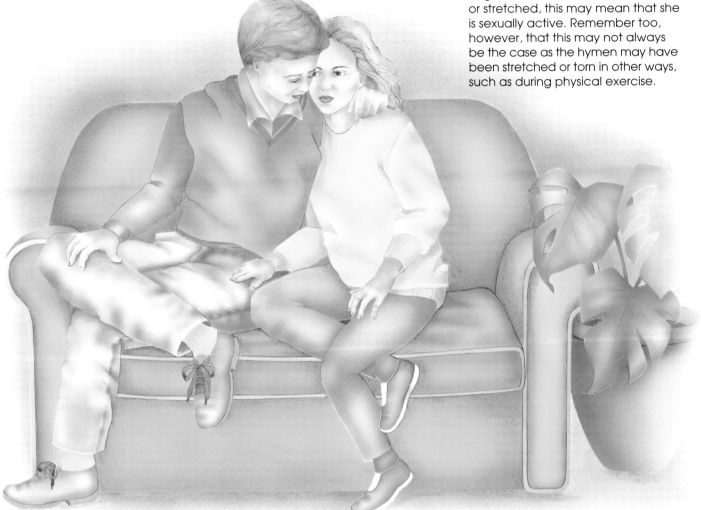

What's love got to do with it?

Love is a strong human emotion and shows itself in different ways. There is the special love you feel for your family and your friends, but there is also the love and powerful sexual attraction you may feel for some-one with whom you want to share your life. Love takes time to develop and means sharing, giving and trusting through good times and bad times. One of the deepest expressions of love is sexual intercourse. This is the closest anyone can get to another person and we should feel comfortable and happy in a strong, committed relation-ship such as marriage before taking this important step towards independence and adulthood.

What is a homosexual?

A homosexual is a man or woman who feels sexually and emotionally attracted to someone of his or her own sex. Although the word 'gay' is often used to describe homosexual men and women, female homosexuals are also known as 'lesbians'. Many heterosexuals (people who are attracted to members of the opposite sex) believe that homosexuality is wrong, while others accept gay people and their lifestyle. It is important to remember that homosexuals have the same needs and feelings as heterosexuals, and a person's sexuality should not be considered a reflection of how 'good' or 'bad' that person is.

Contraception

Having a baby can be a wonderful experience, but sometimes it is best to wait before starting a family. Contraception allows people to choose when they would like to have a baby. It is also very important to remember that casual sex without any form of contraception is irresponsible and can lead to an unwanted pregnancy and many other problems.

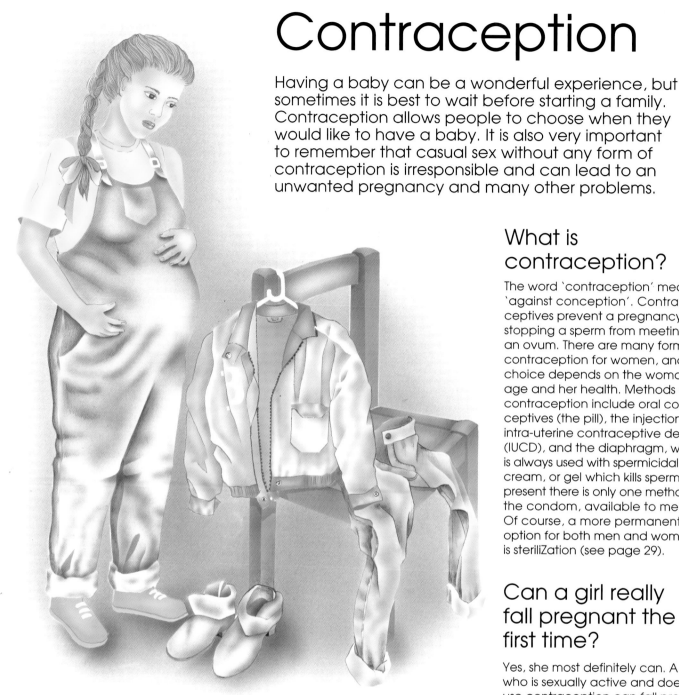

What is contraception?

The word 'contraception' means 'against conception'. Contraceptives prevent a pregnancy by stopping a sperm from meeting with an ovum. There are many forms of contraception for women, and the choice depends on the woman's age and her health. Methods of contraception include oral contraceptives (the pill), the injection, the intra-uterine contraceptive device (IUCD), and the diaphragm, which is always used with spermicidal foam, cream, or gel which kills sperm. At present there is only one method, the condom, available to men. Of course, a more permanent option for both men and women is sterilization (see page 29).

Can a girl really fall pregnant the first time?

Yes, she most definitely can. A girl who is sexually active and does not use contraception can fall pregnant any time after puberty. An understanding of the female reproductive cycle can help you realise that trying to prevent a pregnancy by drinking water and urinating after sexual intercourse, withdrawing the penis before ejaculation, or having sex in different positions, are simply myths and none of these methods have ever been known to prevent a pregnancy. Unprotected sexual intercourse is always a great risk and can cause much heartache in both young people and their families.

Why do we need contraception?

To avoid an unwanted pregnancy. Over the years, there have been many different methods of contraception. Some are successful in preventing a pregnancy, but others are merely myths. Today there are modern, reliable methods of contraception which have few risks or side effects. People use contraceptives so that they can avoid a pregnancy. They may also want to plan their families carefully. Before they take on the responsibilities of being a parent, people need to be financially secure and emotionally mature. They need to decide how long to wait after having their first child before having another. They may also decide not to have any more children at all. These are just some of the reasons why all people who are sexually active should use contraceptives.

What is a condom?

A condom is a thin rubber sheath which fits over the man's erect penis and is thrown away after sexual intercourse. It acts as a contraceptive by keeping the sperm in the sheath and preventing sperm from entering the woman's vagina. It also has a very important use in the prevention of sexually transmitted diseases (see page 30) as it helps stop infection passing between two sexual partners.

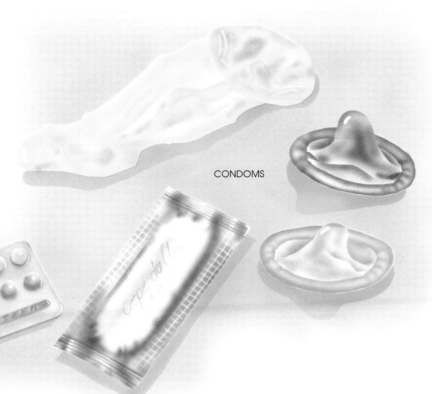

CONDOMS

THE PILL

How does the pill work?

The pill is one of the most widely used and reliable contraceptives, although, like many other contraceptives, there is always the chance that a pregnancy may occur. It is produced in packets of 28 pills made up of female hormones oestrogen and progesterone. A pill is taken every day during the menstrual cycle – whether the woman is having sexual intercourse or not. In this way, the woman's body does not produce an ovum, and she cannot fall pregnant.

Did you know?

Abortion is the purposeful termination of a pregnancy, and is illegal in South Africa and many other countries. Abortion is only allowed when there are serious medical reasons why the woman cannot have the baby, or in cases of incest or rape (see page 25).

What is sterilization?

Sterilization is an operation which can be performed on both men and women so that they are no longer able to have any children. Male sterilization is called vasectomy and involves the closing off of the two tubes, called the vas deferens, which carry sperm into the urethra. A man who has been sterilized is still able to ejaculate but no sperm will be present in the semen. When a woman is sterilized, her fallopian tubes are tied off and cut so that an ovum and a sperm cannot meet. The woman will menstruate as usual. Although they are unable to have a baby, both a man and woman can still enjoy sexual intercourse once they have been sterilized.

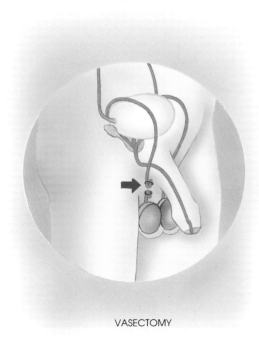

VASECTOMY

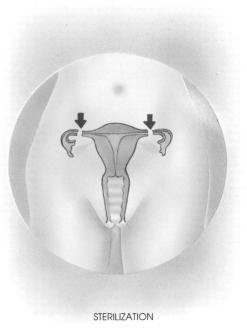

STERILIZATION

Aids and other diseases

One of the dangers associated with sexual intercourse, particularly for those who have more than one sexual partner, is the spreading of sexually transmitted diseases. Although most of these can be cured, many can be very dangerous if left untreated. One of these diseases, AIDS, always leads to death and there is still no known cure.

What are sexually transmitted diseases?

A sexually transmitted disease (STD) is one in which the infection is passed on from one person to another during sexual intercourse and intimacy. There are many different sexually transmitted diseases. Some STDs affect both sexes while others affect only men or only women. Most of these diseases can cause itching, discharge, rashes, or small sores and even blisters in the genital area, but although some may have no clear or visible symptoms at all, they are all infectious. Using a condom (see page 29) is one of the few ways we have to help prevent the spread of STDs, but it is our own responsible behaviour and self-respect that determines how vulnerable we are to these diseases.

How do you get AIDS?

The HIV virus is found in the blood, semen, and vaginal fluids of an infected person. The most common way AIDS is transmitted is through sexual intercourse, but anyone who comes into contact with infected blood will also be at risk. It is therefore very important not to handle the blood of other people. Drug users can also get AIDS by using an infected needle. Although the rapid spread of AIDS is quite scary, it is important to know that you cannot catch AIDS the way you would measles or a cold. You cannot contract the virus by touching a person who has AIDS nor by everyday contact such as sharing toilet facilities, eating from the same plate or swimming in a pool used by an AIDS-sufferer. You also cannot contract AIDS from a mosquito bite.

1

2

3

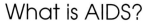

1. White blood cells fight disease

2. HIV kills the white blood cells

3. Secondary diseases attack the body

What is AIDS?

AIDS (Acquired Immune Deficiency Syndrome) is a sexually transmitted disease caused by the HIV virus. The virus may be present in the body for some time before showing any symptoms. The HIV virus attacks the body's white blood cells which protect it against infection. As a result, the body can no longer fight infections. A small cut in a HIV-positive person, for example, will not heal and may become infected. Sometimes even a common cold could turn into pneumonia and the person may die.

Can STDs be cured?

Most sexually transmitted diseases can be cured if discovered early enough. But a person can be reinfected and will have to be treated for the disease once again. STDs such as gonorrhoea, syphilis and chlamydia can be cured but they can also cause infertility. If left unchecked, some STDs can damage the nervous system and cause other serious health problems. Among those for which there is no known cure are genital herpes and AIDS.

Who can I talk to about my problems?

Problems are always made much easier when they are shared with someone. Just talking about something that is bothering you may help you to think it through and come to some solution of your own. Adolescence brings with it some fears and anxieties, and your parents and teachers are always there to help you through these. If you feel you may need outside help, you could contact a local clinic or a professional counselling service.

Index

A
abortion 29
abuse 25
adolescence 16, 18, 19, 20, 21, 22, 23, 31
adulthood 14, 16, 22, 27, 30
advice 25, 26, 31
AIDS **30**, 31
alcohol **7**, 23
amniotic fluid 6, 9
amniotic sac 6, 8, 13
anorexia 15

B
bathing 15, **25**
birth **8**, 9, 10
  mark 11
brain **26**
breastfeeding **10**, 19
breasts 7, 10, 17, **19**
bulimia 15

C
Caesar, Julius 9
caesarian section 9
cancer 23
cell division **5**
cervix 8, 18
Childline **31**
chromosomes **12**, 13
cigarettes **7**, 23
circumcision **21**
clitoris 18, 24
clothes **23**
communication 11, 14, 22, 23
conception 5
condom 28, **29**, 30
contraception 28, **29**, 30
contraceptives 28, **29**

D
dagga 23
diet 15
disease 29, 30, 31
Down's Syndrome 13
drugs **7**, 23, 30

E
eating disorder 15
egg cell **4**, 5
ejaculation 5, 16, 21, 29
embryo 5, 13
emotion 16, 19, 22, 23, 26, 27
endocrine gland **16**
erection 20, 21
exercise 15, 27

F
fallopian tube 4, **18**, 29
fertilization **4**, 5, **6**, **13**
fetus **5**, **6**, **7**, **8**, 9
fontanelle **11**
foreskin 20, 21
friends 22, 23, 27

G
gay 27
genes **12**

genitals 16, 17, **18**, 20, 24, 25, 30
growth 11, 14, 15
guilt 25

H
hair 15, 16, 17
health 14, 15, 23, 30, 31
height 14
Helpline **31**
hereditary disease 12
herpes 31
heterosexual 27
HIV virus 30
homosexual 27
hormones 7, 12, 16, 17, 23, 24, 26, 29
hygiene 15
hymen 18, 27
hypothalamus **26**

I
incest 29
incubator **9**
independence 14, **22**, **23**, 24, 27
infection 7, 10, 29, 30, 31
infertility 23, 31
intercourse **4**, 25, 27, 28, 29, 30, 31

L
labour **8**
  pain 9
larynx 16
lesbian 27
love 4, 27

M
marriage 4, 19, 27
masturbation 24
maturity 14, 16, 19, 22, 23, 26, 27, 28, 30, 31
menstrual cycle **19**
menstruation 4, 6, 17, **19**, 29
milk 7, 10, 19
  formula 10
miscarriage 7
moods 22, 23

N
nocturnal emission 21
nutrients 15

O
oestrogen 7, 16, 17, 29
orgasm 21
ovary 4, **18**
ovulation **19**
ovum **4**, 5, 6, **13**, 17, 28, 29

P
paedophile 25
parents 4, 26
peer pressure 22, 23
pelvis 9, 18, 19
penis **4**, 20, **21**, 24, 29
periods 6, 17, **19**
pill 28, **29**
pimples 17
pituitary gland **26**
placenta **6**, 7, 8

pornography 25
pregnancy 6, **7**, **8**, 9, 19, 28, 29
privacy 24, 25
problems 15, 24, 31
progesterone 7, 16, 29
prostate gland 20, 21
puberty 4, 15, 16, 17, 18, 19, 20, 21, 22, 23, 25, 26
pubic hair 16, 17, 18

R
rape 25, 29
relationships 26, 27
reproductive system **18**, **19**, **20**, **21**
  boy **20**, **21**
  girl **18**, **19**
respect 24, 30
responsibility 14, 19, 22, 23, 27, 28, 30

S
Safeline **31**
sanitary pad 19
scrotum 20
sebaceous gland **17**
sebum 17
semen **4**, 21, 29
seminal fluid 20, 21
seminal vesicle 20, 21
sexual abuse 25
sexual intercourse **4**, 25, 27, 28, 29, 30, 31
sexuality 26, 27
sexually transmitted disease 29, 30, 31
shaving 16
Siamese twins 13
skin 11, 15, **17**
skull **11**
smoking **7**, **23**
sperm **4**, 5, 6, **13**, 16, 20, 21, 28, 29
sterilization 28, **29**
sweat 15, 17
  gland 15, **17**

T
tampon 19
testes 4, 20, **21**
testosterone 16
twins **13**
  Siamese 13

U
umbilical cord **6**, 7, 8
urethra 18, 20, **21**, 29
urine 18, 28
uterus 4, **6**, 7, **8**, 9, **18**, 19

V
vagina **4**, 8, 9, **18**, 29
vaginal fluid 30
vaginal opening 18
vasectomy **29**
virgin 27
vulva 18

W
weight 14
wet dream 16, 21
white blood cells 30